A Prayerbook of
Christian
Belief
STEPS
INTO LIGHT

Ave Maria Press
Notre Dame, Indiana 46556

A Prayerbook of Christian Belief
STEPS INTO LIGHT

Rev. James W. Lyons

Acknowledgment:

Excerpts from the text of THE NEW AMERICAN BIBLE © 1970 by the Confraternity of Christian Doctrine are used by permission of copyright owner.

Nihil Obstat:

    David Burrell, C.S.C.
    Censor Deputatus

Imprimatur:

    William E. McManus
    Bishop of Fort Wayne-South Bend

Library of Congress Catalog Card Number: 78-50791

International Standard Book Number: 0-87793-149-6

Photography: Jean-Claude Lejeune, 2, 3, 10, 15, 20, 26, 56; Notre Dame Printing and Publications Office, 63; Rick Smolan, cover, 32, 42.

Printed in the United States of America.

Contents

Preface

One spring morning I was making my chaplain visitations at Palos Community Hospital. I can recall visiting an elderly patient in Room 434, bed 2. He made a very simple and sincere request. "I've had a lot of time to think things over. I want to learn about religion. I want to believe in something worthwhile. Could you give me something to read?"

"I'll get just what you need," I replied.

As I left the room and walked down the fourth-floor corridor to the elevator I thought, I'd need a small book with large print that would present the basic teachings of religion in a simple, prayerful and biblical manner. I soon realized that there was no book like that. I would have to write it myself.

This book is the result of the request made by the patient in Room 434-2 at Palos Community Hospital. I am grateful to Father John Reedy, editor of Ave Maria Press, for convincing me that while this booklet would be of value to hospital patients, it will also be helpful to any person who is searching for a simple introduction to the basic truths of faith. It was not my intent to include every religious truth in this booklet, but simply a few basic truths. Each truth is linked with an appropriate prayer so that the reader may learn while praying, and pray while learning.

It is my prayer that this book may be responsible for the birth of faith in many hearts. It is simple and sufficiently short to be read frequently. It is my hope that each time it is read the reader will attain greater faith in God, in himself and in others. To suit our purpose various translations of the Holy Scriptures have been used.

Speak, Lord, for your servant is listening (1 Sm 3:10).*

You have the words of eternal life (Jn 6:68).

---

*Except when otherwise indicated, quotations from scripture are from The New American Bible.

ÿ

Introduction

Slow Me Down

Socrates in the *Apology* said that we should not merely live, but we should live well. To live well we must take occasional time-outs in order to reflect and to pray. Isaiah wrote:

> The Sovereign Lord, the holy One of Israel, says to the people, "Come back and quietly trust in me. Then you will be strong and secure." But you refuse to do it. Instead, you plan to escape from your enemies by riding fast horses. And you are right—escape is what you will have to do! You think your horses are fast enough, but those who pursue you will be faster! A thousand of you will run away when you see one enemy soldier, and five soldiers will be enough to make you all run away. Nothing will be left of your army except a lonely flagpole on the top of a hill. And yet the Lord is waiting to be merciful to you. He is ready to take pity on you because he always does what is right. Happy are those who put their trust in the Lord (Is 30:15-18—GNB).

Let us ask God to slow us down:

Slow me down, Lord!

Steady my hurried pace with a vision of the eternal reach of time.

Teach me the art of taking minute vacations,

Of slowing down to look at a flower . . . to chat with an old friend . . . or to make a new one . . . to pat a stray dog . . . to watch a spider spin a gossamer web . . . to smile at a child . . . or to read a few lines from a good book.

Remind me each day that the race is not always to the swift;

That there is more to life than increasing its speed.

Slow me down, Lord!

Inspire me to send my roots deep into the soil of life's enduring values.

(Orin Crain)

Some are strong in chariots; some, in horses;
but we are strong in the name of the Lord, our God
(Ps 20:8).

"Come back and quietly trust in me. Then you will be strong and secure," says the Lord (Is 30:15— GNB).

I. The Light of Conscience

Lead, Kindly Light

When we slow down and all is peaceful we can ascend to God. "For all men were by nature foolish who were in ignorance of God, and who from the good things seen did not succeed in knowing him who is, and from studying the works did not discern the artisan" (Wis 13:1).

"Since the creation of the world, invisible realities, God's eternal power and divinity, have become visible, recognized through the things he has made" (Rom 1:20). We become aware of the power, the goodness and the beauty of God in creation — in the mountains and lakes, in the flowers and animals, in our powers to think and to love, and in our consciences. How easy it is to hear the voice of God in the sanctuary of our consciences!

Lead, Kindly Light, amid the encircling gloom
    Lead thou me on!
The night is dark, and I am far from home —
    Lead thou me on!
Keep thou my feet; I do not ask to see
    The distant scene — one step enough for me.
I was not ever thus, nor pray'd that thou
    Shouldst lead me on;
I loved to choose and see my path, but now
    Lead thou me on!
I loved the garish day, and, spite of fears,
    Pride ruled my will: remember not past years.
So long thy power hath blest me, sure it still
    Will lead me on.
O'er moor and fen, o'er crag and torrent, till
    The night is gone;
And with the morn those angel faces smile
    Which I have loved long since, and lost awhile.
                  (John Henry Newman)

O God, how pleasant it is to think about you! The very thought of you makes me aware of infinite love and perfect existence. Help me always to be aware of your divine power and goodness reflected in all creatures. Help me always to listen to your kindly voice as you speak to me in my conscience.

Behold, you are pleased with sincerity of heart, and in my inmost being you teach me wisdom (Ps 51:8).

A Little Less Than the Angels

In creating us God has placed us above all other earthly creatures. He has given us the ability to think, to be conscientious, to reason, to communicate. How good God has been to each of us!

O Lord, our Lord,
   how glorious is your name over all the earth!
   You have exalted your majesty above the heavens.
Out of the mouths of babes and sucklings
   you have fashioned praise because of your foes,
   to silence the hostile and the vengeful.
When I behold your heavens, the work of your fingers,
   the moon and the stars which you set in place—
What is man that you should be mindful of him;
   or the son of man that you should care for him?

You have made him little less than the angels,
   and crowned him with glory and honor.
You have given him rule over the works of your hands,
   putting all things under his feet;
All sheep and oxen,
   yes, and the beasts of the field,
The birds of the air and the fishes of the sea,
   and whatever swims the paths of the seas.
O Lord, our Lord,
   how glorious is your name over all the earth!

(Psalm 8)

O God, how wonderful you have been to me to give me consciousness, to give me conscience and the ability to think, to reason, to understand, to perceive and to speak. Help me never to abuse these gifts. Help me to use these gifts to come closer to you, and to bring others into the warmth and sunshine of your love. Amen.

Man, for all his splendor, if he have not prudence, resembles the beasts that perish (Ps 49:21).

The Laws of Love

Since God is our creator, he knows how we should live and love. To help us have happy lives and love properly, God has given us the Ten Commandments to inform our consciences.

1. I, the Lord, am your God. You shall not have other gods beside me.
2. You shall not take the name of the Lord, your God, in vain.
3. Remember to keep holy the sabbath day.
4. Honor your father and your mother.
5. You shall not kill.
6. You shall not commit adultery.
7. You shall not steal.
8. You shall not bear false witness against your neighbor.
9. You shall not covet your neighbor's wife.
10. You shall not covet your neighbor's goods.

(Ex 20:1-17)

These laws were not given to harm us but to help us, to help us perfect our human nature, to live a life of serenity and joy. They reach into the roots of our existence, where we form the primary relationships of our lives, and then we are established firmly in God.

O Lord, I thank you for giving me your holy laws.
May I avoid sin and always follow your holy laws.
May I see your goodness and love expressed in these
    divine laws.
May I find serenity and joy in following these holy
    laws. Amen.

I long for your salvation, O Lord,
    and your law is my delight (Ps 119:174).

II. The Light of Faith in Christ

Our Need for God

As we strive to follow the voice of God in our consciences and try to fulfill God's plan for us, we at times become discouraged. We fall into sins and need help. We live in the expectation of a divine revelation. We live in semidarkness. We are similar to the prisoners in Plato's *Republic* who lived in a cave with only the light of a candle to aid their vision. Finally, they are released, and climb up to the sunlight. What wonders do they see! The miracles and prophecies of Holy Scripture, the word of God and the love among Christians indicate that Christ is our light, our helper, our Savior.

Through observation and the use of reason we can learn about some religious truths such as the existence of God, attributes such as his power, goodness and reason, and the immortality of the soul. Through revelation these truths can be clarified.

Other truths can be learned only through revelation. Among these are the divinity of Christ and the mystery of three persons in one God, the Holy Trinity.

Through revelation and faith we are taught that God loved us so much that he gave his Son as our redeemer, and the Son so loved us that he gave his life for our salvation.

Jesus, Our Savior
One Solitary Life

He was born in an obscure village, the child of a peasant woman. He grew up in still another village, where he worked in a carpenter's shop until he was 30. Then for three years he was an itinerant preacher. He never wrote a book, never held an office, never had a family or owned a house. He didn't go to college. He never visited a big city, never traveled 200 miles from the place where he was born. He did none of the things one usually associates with greatness. He had no credentials but himself.

He was only 33 when the tide of public opinion turned against him. His friends ran away. He was turned over to his enemies and went through the mockery of a trial. He was nailed to a cross between two thieves. While he was dying, his executioners gambled for his clothing, the only property he had on earth. When he was dead, he was laid in a grave given through the pity of a friend.

Nineteen centuries have come and gone, and today he is the central figure of the human race and the leader of mankind's progress. All the armies that ever marched, all the navies that ever sailed, all the parliaments that ever sat, all the kings that ever reigned, put together, have not affected the life of man on this earth as much as that *one solitary life*.

(Author Unknown)

O Jesus, you came not to abolish the laws of God, but to fulfill them.

Give me the serenity and joy that you had in your holy home with your mother Mary and your foster-father, Joseph.

Help me not to live for wealth, for recognition, for prestige, for power.

Help me to give my life for truth, for goodness, for love.

Help me to give my life to you.

(James W. Lyons)

A lamp to my feet is your word,
a light to my path (Ps 119:105).

Christ Be with Me

As we follow the voice of God in our consciences and keep the commandments, at times we are aware of our limitations. We need help. We must give ourselves completely to Christ in faith. In Jesus Christ the Son of God we have all the aid that we need. Our faith should be centered in Christ. He is our way, our truth and our life.

Christ be with me, Christ within me,
Christ behind me, Christ before me,
Christ beside me, Christ to win me.
Christ to comfort and restore me,
Christ beneath me, Christ above me,
Christ in quiet, Christ in danger,
Christ in hearts of all that love me,
Christ in mouth of friends and stranger.

(St. Patrick)

I will proclaim the decree of the Lord.
The Lord said to me, "You are my son;
   this day I have begotten you" (Ps 2:7).

Jesus Died for Us

Jesus died on the cross because he loved us and wanted to save us from our sins. There is much to be learned from books but as St. Thomas Aquinas said, the greatest book was the crucifix.

Look down upon me, good and gentle Jesus, while before your face I humbly kneel and, with burning soul, pray and beseech you to fix deep in my heart lively sentiments of faith, hope and charity, true contrition for my sins and a firm purpose of amendment.

While I contemplate, with great love and tender pity, your five most precious wounds, pondering over them within me and calling to mind the word which David your prophet said of you, my Jesus.

"They have pierced my hands and my feet; they have numbered all my bones (Ps 22:17)."

(St. Thomas Aquinas)

The Darkness of Sin

God knew that in spite of all our spiritual resources, there would be times when we would fall into sin. But he did not want us to be discouraged or filled with self-contempt. He wanted us to trust in his love and mercy. To illustrate the love and mercy God shows to us even though we sin, Christ told us the parable of the prodigal son:

A man had two sons. The younger son asked for his share of the property and upon receiving it left home for a distant country. He spent all of the money. When a famine came, he went to work caring for pigs. Then coming to his senses he returned to the home of his father. Seeing his son off in the distance, the father ran up and welcomed him home (See Lk 15).

God our Father, just as the father forgave his
    prodigal son, forgive my sins.

Heal me from the sickness of my sins.

Reconcile me to yourself, O God, and to our
    community of love.

Give me the humility to admit my failures and
    sins.

Give me faith and trust in your everlasting
    mercy.

(James W. Lyons)

Have mercy on me, O God, in your goodness;
    in the greatness of your compassion wipe out
    my offense (Ps 51:1).

Sorrow for Sin

We should tell God frequently that we are sorry for our sins because we love him. When we turn to him he will forgive us. The Lord says, "Now, let's settle the matter. You are stained red with sin, but I will wash you as clean as snow. Although your stains are deep red, you will be as white as wool. If you will only obey me, you will eat the good things the land produces. But if you defy me, you are doomed to die. I, the Lord, have spoken" (Is 1:18-20).

O my God, I am heartily sorry for having
offended thee,
And I detest all my sins, because of thy just
punishments,
But most of all because they offend thee, my
God, who art all good and deserving of
all my love.
I firmly resolve, with the help of thy grace, to
confess my sins, to do penance, to sin no
more and to avoid the near occasions of
sin. Amen.

Have mercy on me, O God, in your goodness;
in the greatness of your compassion wipe
out my offense.
Thoroughly wash me from my guilt
and of my sin cleanse me (Ps 51:3, 4).

The Healing of Memories

When we are truly sorry for our sins God forgives us. God therefore expects us to be willing to forgive others. To teach us to forgive others, Christ told the parable about the servant who owed his master a vast sum of money. When the servant pleaded with the master, the master forgave his debt. But then the servant went out and met another servant who owed him only a few dollars, and he began to beat him for not paying the debt. When the master heard about this, he punished the ungrateful servant. Christ concluded by saying, "That is how my Father in heaven will treat you if you do not forgive your brother, every one of you, from your heart" (Mt 17).

Merciful Father, you have always forgiven my sins
    when I was truly sorry.
I am grateful for your healing power which has
    helped me physically, mentally, and spiritually.
I ask that you give me the help of your grace so that
    I will forgive others.
Come, Lord Jesus. Heal my miserable memories.
Come, O Holy Spirit, and halt the old broken records
    of unpleasant memories.
Give me the strength to forgive and to forget.

(James W. Lyons)

Kindness and truth shall meet,
    justice and peace shall kiss (Ps 85:11).

III. The Light of
the Spirit

Our Teacher

The night before he died, Christ told us that he would not leave us orphans. To help us to understand his teaching and to live his life, he has sent the Holy Spirit to guide our hearts and our Church.

"The Spirit too helps us in our weakness, for we do not know how to pray as we ought; but the Spirit makes intercession for us with groanings that cannot be expressed in speech. He who searches hearts knows what the Spirit means, for the Spirit intercedes for the saints as God himself wills" (Rom 8:26-27).

O Holy Spirit of our Lord Jesus Christ, come to us.

Teach us all that Jesus wants us to know.

Guide and inspire our community of love, our Church.

Help us to understand that there should never be a conflict between the Spirit teaching in our Church and the Spirit teaching in our individual hearts since the same Spirit guides us as a community and as individuals.

Help us, O Holy Spirit, to have a deep appreciation of the presence of your warmth and peace.

(James W. Lyons)

Where can I go from your Spirit?
from your presence where can I flee?
If I go up to the heavens, you are there;
if I sink to the nether world, you are present there (Ps 139:7, 8).

Lord, I Believe

Many truths about our lives can only be learned through the revelation of Christ. Such truths cannot be seen, nor can they be proven scientifically, but since they came from God, we know that they should be believed. These truths we accept on faith. Today many people are involved in a crisis of faith. We should pray for faith in God and faith in the Spirit working in the community of love, his Church.

Lord, I believe; I wish to believe in thee.

Lord, let my faith be full and unreserved, and let it penetrate my thought, my way of judging divine things and human things.

Lord, let my faith be joyful and give peace and gladness to my spirit, and dispose it for prayer with God and conversation with men, so that the inner bliss of its fortunate possession may shine forth in sacred and secular conversation.

Lord, let my faith be humble and not presume to be based on the experience of my thought and of my feeling, but let it surrender to the testimony of the Holy Spirit, and not have any better guarantee than in docility to tradition and to the authority of the magisterium of Holy Church. Amen. (Paul VI)

Happy the man who makes the Lord his trust,
 who turns not to idolatry
 or to those who stray after falsehood (Ps 40:5).

The Trinity

Speaking to us as individuals and in our Church, the Holy Spirit teaches us many truths. One of these is that there are three persons in one God. They are God the Father, God the Son and God the Holy Spirit.

May the voice of God the Father in our consciences,
The light of the Spirit in our hearts,
And the light of the Spirit in the faith of our fathers
and mothers, enable us to follow the Son, our
brother.
May this joyful journey of love with the Way, the
Truth and the Life lead us to eternal life. Amen.
(James W. Lyons)

A clean heart create for me, O God,
and a steadfast spirit renew within me.
Cast me not out from your presence,
and your Holy Spirit take not from me.
Give me back the joy of your salvation
and a willing spirit sustain in me (Ps 51:12-14).

Saying Yes to God

It may be easy or it may be difficult. We may be praised or we may be criticized—but always we try to do the will of God as he speaks to us in our consciences and guides us with his Holy Spirit. This is how God tells us what is good.

"You have been told, O man, what is good,
and what the Lord requires of you:
Only to do right and to love goodness,
and to walk humbly with your God" (Mi 6-8).

Dear Lord, teach me to be generous; teach me to
serve you as you deserve,
To give and not count the cost,
To fight and not heed the wounds,
To toil and not seek for rest,
To labor and not seek reward,
Save that of knowing that I do your will.

(St. Ignatius)

Bless the Lord, O my soul;
and all my being, bless his holy name (Ps 103:1).

Happiness in the Spirit

Doing the will of God and acting through the grace of Christ under the inspiration of the Holy Spirit, we find a sweetness and a joy in our hearts. In spite of adverse incidents and circumstances, we discover a happiness that the world cannot give. In the Sermon on the Mount Jesus spoke about this happiness or beatitude. He said:

Blessed are the poor in spirit,
> for theirs is the kingdom of heaven.

Blessed are the meek,
> for they shall possess the earth.

Blessed are they who mourn,
> for they shall be comforted.

Blessed are they who hunger and thirst for justice,
> for they shall have their fill.

Blessed are the merciful,
> for they shall obtain mercy.

Blessed are the clean of heart,
> for they shall see God.

Blessed are the peacemakers,
> for they shall be called the children of God.

Blessed are they who suffer persecution for justice' sake, for theirs is the kingdom of heaven (Mt 5:3-10—DR).

O Holy Spirit, who dwells within us as our friend and companion, fill us with your divine gifts. Fill our hearts with your gifts of wisdom, understanding, counsel, fortitude, knowledge, piety, and fear of the Lord so that in days of storms or in days of sunshine we may walk in peace, in hope and in joy.

(James W. Lyons)

Taste and see how good the Lord is;
happy the man who takes refuge in him (Ps 34:9).

IV. The Light of Love

Instruments of Peace

It is important for us to avoid sin, but we do not wish to be merely negative in the service of God. God wants each of us to be instruments of his peace and love. The best way to stay out of sin is to love properly. Christ summarized all of the laws and prophecies by saying:

"You must love the Lord your God
with all your heart,
with all your soul,
with all your strength,
and with all your mind;
and your neighbor as yourself" (Lk 10:27).

44

Lord, make me an instrument of your peace.
Where there is hatred, let me sow love;
Where there is injury, pardon;
Where there is doubt, faith;
Where there is despair, hope;
Where there is darkness, light;
Where there is sadness, joy.
O Divine Master, grant that I may not so much seek
to be consoled as to console;
To be understood, as to understand;
To be loved, as to love.
For it is by giving that we receive;
By pardoning that we are pardoned,
And by dying that we are born into eternal
life in thee. (St. Francis of Assisi)

May the Spirit of our Lord Jesus Christ help us always to be instruments of his peace.

Happy is he who has regard for the lowly and the poor; in the day of misfortune the Lord will deliver him (Ps 41:1).

Prayer for Peace

God wants us to pray and to work for peace in ourselves, in our homes, in our communities, in our nation and throughout the world. It is the will of God that all of the wounds caused by hatred, be healed.

May God banish from the hearts of men whatever might endanger peace. May God transform men into witnesses of truth, justice and brotherly love. May God enlighten the rulers of peoples so that they may formulate and accept a world governed by laws that are just. Finally, may God enkindle the wills of all, so that they may overcome the barriers that divide, cherish the bonds of mutual charity, understand others, and pardon those who have done them wrong. By virtue of God's action may all peoples of the earth become as brothers, and may the most longed for peace blossom forth and reign always between them.

(John XXIII)

As we work for peace and unity among political, ethnic and religious communities we should keep in mind the words of St. Augustine: "In essentials unity, in accidentals diversity, in all things charity."

Watch the wholehearted man, and mark the upright, for there is a future for the man of peace (Ps 37:37).

More and More Like Jesus

As we practice works of love and grow in the grace of Christ, we become more and more like Jesus. We pray that our lives will always reflect the life and love of Jesus. "We are an aroma of Christ for God's sake, both among those who are being saved, and those on the way to destruction" (2 Cor 2:15).

Dear Jesus, help me to spread thy fragrance
    everywhere.

Flood my soul with thy Spirit and thy life.

Penetrate and possess my whole being so utterly that
    all of my life may be only a radiance of thine.

Shine through me and be so in me that every soul I
    come in contact with may feel thy presence
    within me.

Let them look up and see no longer me, but only
    Jesus.

                         (John Henry Newman)

I said: you are gods,
    all of you sons of the Most High (Ps 82:6).

Meaning in My Life

As I listen to the voice of God in my conscience and emulate the life of Jesus, how wonderful it is for me to realize that there is a special meaning and purpose in my life! I am needed; I am wanted; I am a significant part of God's plan. In the body of Christ each of us has a specific mission, a special task to perform.

God has created me to do him some definite service;

He has committed some work to me which he has not committed to another.

I have my mission—I may never know it in this life, but I shall be told it in the next.

I am a link in a chain, a bond of connection between persons.

He has not created me for naught.

I shall do good.

I shall do his work.

I shall be an angel of peace, a preacher of truth in my own place while not intending it—if I do but keep his commandments.

Whatever, wherever I am, I can never be thrown away.

If I am in sickness, my sickness may serve him.

He does nothing in vain.

He knows what he is about.

He may take away my friends; he may throw me among strangers; he may make me feel desolate, make my spirits sink, hide my future from me— still he knows what he is about.

Therefore, I will trust him.

(John Henry Newman)

Enlighten me, O Holy Spirit, that I may know the work that you wish me to do. Help me to develop the gifts that you have given to me. Strengthen me, that I may faithfully and loyally serve you and others in my work. Amen.

(James W. Lyons)

Truly you have formed my inmost being;
   you knit me in my mother's womb (Ps 139:13).

Serenity, Courage and Wisdom

As we try to follow God's plan for us,
we must become realistic.
We should not become skeptics believing that everything
    is corrupt
and should be changed;
nor should we become stoics
and believe that as things are
things should always remain.
There are great traditions
and ways of life to which we should adhere,
and these should not be changed.
But there are also things that should be changed,
and among these are things that we can change,
and other things that are beyond us.

Therefore we pray:

God grant me the serenity to accept
    the things I cannot change,
Courage to change the things I can,
And the wisdom to know the difference.
                              (Reinhold Niebuhr)

As soon as I lie down, I fall peacefully asleep,
    for you alone, O Lord,
        bring security to my dwelling (Ps 4:9).

God Watches Over Us

God not only created us, but he watches over us, helps us to avoid sin and to love others. He does not want us to be filled with worries and anxieties.

Jesus told us, "Consider the lilies of the field, how they grow; they toil not, neither do they spin; And yet I tell you, even Solomon in all his glory was not arrayed like one of these. But if God so clothes the grass of the field, which today is alive and tomorrow is thrown into the oven, will he not much more clothe you, O men of little faith?" (Mt 6:28-30—RSV).

Through his loving providential care he guides us into eternal life. May we accept his guidance!

The Lord is my shepherd;
    I shall not want.
He makes me lie down in green pastures.
    He leads me beside still waters;
He restores my soul.
    He leads me in the paths of righteousness
        for his name's sake.
Even though I walk through the valley of the
        shadow of death,
    I fear no evil;
    For thou art with me;
    Thy rod and thy staff, they comfort me.
Thou preparest a table before me
        in the presence of my enemies;
    Thou anointest my head with oil,
    My cup overflows.
Surely goodness and mercy shall follow me
        all the days of my life;
And I shall dwell in the house of the Lord
        forever.

                (Psalm 23—RSV)

Hope in the Lord

While on earth, as we try to do the work God has given us, we experience smooth and sunny days. But we also encounter days that are rough and stormy. Like Jesus we will suffer. If we hope and trust in the Lord, we shall always experience the peace of Christ and find goodness even in what is difficult and hurtful.

They that hope in the Lord will renew their strength.
They will soar as with eagles' wings,
They will run and not grow weary,
Walk and not grow faint.

(Isaiah 40:31)

Help me, O Lord, to be willing to suffer with you.
Help me to understand that just as out of your death came the resurrection, so also can goodness result from my suffering.
Even during my times of pain and anxiety may I be willing to count the many blessings that I have received from your generous and gracious hands.

(James W. Lyons)

The Lord is close to the brokenhearted;
and those who are crushed in spirit he saves
(Ps 34:19).

Peace at Last

O Lord,
    support us all the day long
        of this life,
    until the shadows lengthen,
    and the evening comes,
    and the busy world is hushed,
    and the fever of life is over,
    and our work is done.
Then, in your mercy,
    grant us a safe lodging and a
        holy rest,
    and peace at the last.

                    (John Henry Newman)

V. The Light of Glory

Through Death

It is never easy for us to experience the death of one whom we have known and loved. The sorrow is great. St. Augustine wrote, "I would not tell you not to weep any more than I would tell you not to love." At the hour of death may we have faith in all that the risen Christ has taught us about heaven. May we have hope that another person has entered heaven and may we continue to love God and others as we proceed to our eternal reunion in heaven.

Almighty and most merciful Father, you know the weakness of my nature.

Bow down your ear in pity to your servant upon whom you have laid the heavy burden of sorrow.

Take away out of my heart the spirit of rebellion, and teach me to see your good and gracious purpose working in all the trials which you send upon me.

Grant that I may not languish in fruitless and unavailing grief, not sorrow as those who have no hope, but through my tears look meekly up to you, the God of all consolation.

Through Christ our Lord. Amen.

(Roman Ritual)

As the hind longs for the running waters,
     so my soul longs for you, O God.
Athirst is my soul for God, the living God (Ps 41:2-3).

From Sorrow to Joy

God is able to turn sorrow into joy, suffering into gain, death into life. "We know that God makes all things work together for the good of those who love him, who have been called according to his decree" (Rom 9:28).

Father, all-powerful and ever-living God,
we do well always and everywhere to give you thanks
through Jesus Christ our Lord.

In him, who rose from the dead,
our hope of resurrection dawned.
The sadness of death gives way
to the bright promise of immortality.

Lord, for your faithful people life is changed, not ended.
When the body of our earthly dwelling lies in death
we gain an everlasting dwelling in heaven.

(Roman Missal)

May we then go forward eagerly to meet the Lord, and
after our life on earth be united with our brothers
and sisters where every tear will be wiped away.
Amen.

One thing I ask of the Lord;
this I seek:
To dwell in the house of the Lord
all the days of my life (Ps 27:4).

Ode to Joy

Because of the good news that Christ has told us about our eternal life with him in heaven, we can be joyful now and always.

Ode to Joy

Sing with all the sons of glory,
Sing the resurrection song!
Death and sorrow, earth's dark story,
To the former days belong.
All around the clouds are breaking,
Soon the storms of time shall cease;
In God's likeness, man awaking,
Knows the everlasting peace.

O what glory, far exceeding
All that eye has yet perceived!
Holiest hearts for ages pleading,
Never that full joy conceived.
God has promised, Christ prepares it,
There on high our welcome waits;
Every humble spirit shares it,
Christ has passed the eternal gates.

Life eternal! Heaven rejoices:
Jesus lives who once was dead;
Join, O man, the deathless voices;
Child of God, lift up thy head!
Patriarchs from the distant ages,
Saints all longing for their heaven,
Prophets, psalmists, seers, and sages,
All await the glory given.

Life eternal! O what wonders
Crowd on faith; what joy unknown,
When amidst earth's closing thunders,
Saints shall stand before the throne!
O to enter that bright portal,
See that glowing firmament,
Know, with thee, O God immortal,
"Jesus Christ whom thou has sent!"
                    (Schiller. Tr. by W. J. Irons)

Praise God

Lord, you are great and greatly to
    be praised;

Great is your power and your wisdom
    infinite.

We would praise you without ceasing.

You call us to delight in your praise,
    for you have made us for yourself,
    and our hearts are restless until
    they rest in you.

(St. Augustine)

Glory to God in the Highest

Glory to God in the highest
    and peace to his people on earth.
Lord God, heavenly King,
almighty God and Father,
    we worship you, we give you thanks,
    we praise you for your glory.
Lord Jesus Christ, only Son of the Father,
Lord God, Lamb of God,
you take away the sin of the world:
    have mercy on us;
you are seated at the right hand of the Father:
    receive our prayer.
For you alone are the Holy One,
you alone are the Lord,
you alone are the Most High,
    Jesus Christ,
    with the Holy Spirit,
    in the glory of God the Father. Amen.

(Roman Missal)